# Random Wisdom
# Connections

## Reflections for Speakers, Teachers, and Trainers

**John Labbe**

# ▪▪Sagesse

Arlington Heights, IL

To my wife, Karen, who is my friend and constant support. More importantly, she is the most dedicated teacher in my life and an inspiration.

# Contents

Before We Begin                    6

Authenticity                      **12**

Audience                          22

Delivery                          30

Growth                            44

Humor                             56

Truth                             64

Influences                        76

Writing                           88

Your Turn                         98

Index                            102

About the Author                 106

# Acknowledgements

This book would be weaker, less readable, and possibly unfinished without the help and encouragement of many, many friends. When I told Conor Cunneen that I was working on a book about speaking and teaching he became relentless in reminding me to keep writing every time we met. A good mentor will pester you like this, and Conor has been a fine mentor in other ways, too. Likewise, my friend Iqbal Atcha, like Conor a speaker and an author in his own right, proved a persistent and enthusiastic cheerleader. Iqbal particularly helped me believe that the end product would be solid and worth reading. I'm sure most writers need encouragement such as I received from Conor and Iqbal, but I benefited greatly from it.

This book would make almost no sense if I hadn't been able to find ways to link speaking, teaching and training. To this end, I reached out to various speakers, teachers, and trainers for their thoughts and, eventually, their feedback. I'm especially indebted to Amy Atcha, Al Matan, and Virginia Bosserman for their careful readings and thoughtful, candid feedback.

Many other friends offered encouragement and reactions to early draft sections of the book as well. If I named everyone, I fear the book would become more acknowledgement than prose. Thank you all; you know who you are.

# Before We Begin

*"The beginning is always today."*
*—Mary Shelley (Novelist)*

We rarely make the best use of all the lessons that we've learned in our professional experience. Most of those lessons aren't lost to us, they're just buried somewhere in memory. To uncover them, we may need a trigger. I've found that random pieces of wisdom from other disciplines can help me find lost connections to some useful wisdom in my own field of teaching that is lurking in my experience memory.

If my experience is at all typical, you too have probably forgotten a good deal of all that you've learned about your profession. In the relentless doing of our workaday lives, we sometimes let useful lessons fade into memory and drop them from regular use. It just happens over time. Most of those lessons aren't lost to us, they're just buried somewhere in our memory. I've found a trigger that helps me recover them and I hope it will work for you as well.

## The Random Wisdom Method

A few months ago, one of my friends posted to Facebook a quote from Groucho Marx: "I sent the club a wire stating, please accept my resignation. I don't want to belong to any club that will accept me as a member." I'm sure most of us regularly see similar quotes from famous people in our social media feeds and we know our friends mean to inspire us or make us laugh.

In my case, though, when I saw that line from Groucho Marx, I wasn't especially inspired nor particularly amused. Instead, seeing it jogged my memory. I started to think about how membership, or a sense of belonging, can play an important role in learning.

It seems to be a part of human nature to want to be a part of something larger than ourselves. When learning something difficult is essential to belonging to a desirable group, the desire for membership somehow makes the learning easier. Without getting lost in an essay on membership, it was then that I decided to see what other insights into teaching I might jog from my memory by exposing myself to random quotes.

To write this book, I started by selecting about 100 celebrities whose quotes could be found on Internet quote sites. Initially I picked celebrities who were interesting to me. I wanted to find my inspirations from mostly ordinary thinkers. Though I admire Abraham Lincoln more than any other person in history, I chose to avoid using quotes from him or other well-recognized sources of wisdom. You won't find anything here from Mahatma Gandhi or President John Kennedy, or even Thomas Jefferson. I wanted the wisdom to be as random as could be.

After selecting these celebrities, I picked a few quotes from each one that amused or interested me. Some of these prompted me to think about various aspects of teaching, and from these I started writing the reflections that make up this book.

These reflections are all relatively short and none of them is a fully polished essay. In form, they're perhaps closer to a blog post than an essay you might read in a journal. That's intentional. I want you to see the reflective process in motion as you read. For it's in that reflection that the power of the random wisdom method is unleashed.

## About the word *Teacher*

In my life I have taught classes in hotel meeting rooms, high school and college classrooms, and in corporate training centers. I have been a professional speaker, teacher, and trainer most of my adult life. In my view, anyone who works in these three fields is a teacher. So while this book's title calls out speakers, teachers, and trainer, in this book I call them all "teacher" unless there is a need for more clarity.

Teaching simply takes many forms and it does not matter how you acquire your students or what your job title is. Likewise, whether I'm talking about teaching in a classroom or a meeting room, I refer to the rest of the people in those rooms as students.

# How to Read this Book

This is a book of prompted reflections. In reading it, you will see how the quotes I selected prompted me to recall and reflect on important lessons about teaching. The chapters are not sequential, so it's not necessary to read this book from front to back. Instead, I encourage you to start anywhere that appeals to you. Enjoy it. Savor the thoughts about your own work that come to mind as you read. If my thoughts tell you something new or if they amuse you, that's even better.

My reflections for this book tended toward three different results. In some, I found myself recalling how I came to believe in certain teaching techniques and these reflections helped to strengthen my faith in those techniques. Others brought up memories that helped me refine my ideas about teaching, so now I am a better teacher for having done this work. Finally, some of these reflections surprised me and helped me see ways in which I could do things differently as a teacher, ways to improve what I do. For all these results, I am grateful. I hope that you will find similar results when you try your hand at similar reflections.

At the end of the book, you'll find additional quotes, a collection of random wisdom for your own use. These are included for your benefit in the hope that you'll pause to do your own reflecting. Enjoy!

# Before We Begin

# Authenticity

*"You don't have to cook fancy or complicated masterpieces - just good food from fresh ingredients." Julia Child (TV Chef and Cookbook Author)*

The first rule of writing - and this applies to teaching as well - is this: have something valuable to say. Nothing is duller reading than a piece that has no point or does not, in some way, add value to the human conversation. If we're here to both learn and teach (and I believe that this is definitely one of our reasons for being, and not only for those of us who are employed as teachers), then shouldn't we be interested in teaching something of value?

I can't begin to count the number of lectures, speeches and presentations I've heard that had no real point, or whose point was not supported by any useful evidence. It's as if some people think that merely filling an allotted time slot or writing a certain number of words should be enough. It's not.

But, John, you say, I teach high school French. I don't have anything original to say about the passé composé or subject-verb agreement. Sure you do. You have the authority of knowing how the French language works and you have the experience of using it in real life. You know the confusion that incorrect grammar can cause. You probably remember a time when your own mistake sent you to a zoo instead of a washroom when asking for directions in Paris.

What you have to say that is valuable comes from your experience with the language. The same is true for math teachers and sales trainers alike: your personal relationship with your topic is where you will find your fresh ingredients, as Julia Child would say.

Teachers have an obligation to add to the human conversation. If you want to be a motivational speaker, for example, and all you know about motivation comes from what you have read in Zig Ziglar's books, then I think you're going to fail in your endeavor. I can't imagine many audiences being willing to pay for "wisdom" that is just warmed over summaries of readily available books or presentations.

There's a danger in wanting mostly the surface-image of something. By this I mean that it's dangerous to want to have the fruits of a successful career without actually having worked the career. The speaker who, for example, wants to jump into speaking before crowds of a thousand but who has not learned the craft by speaking to rooms of a dozen Rotarians is going to flop. Part of the reason for this, aside from the obvious problems of perfecting delivery and style, is that a message with long-term value takes time to develop and refine. It has to stand up to hours of audience Q and A sessions before you can be sure that it's bullet proof.

*"In order to be irreplaceable one must always be different." Coco Chanel (Fashion designer)*

---

We distrust politicians when they tell dramatic stories of unfortunate citizens. We're supposed to believe that if we elect the speaker, or if Congress will just vote to pass some piece of legislation or other, then the causes of such hardships will disappear. Such terrible things will never ever happen to good people again, or so they want us to think. Rubbish.

I think these stories reveal two problems. I'm always skeptical that things will ever change dramatically with just one election or one new legislative action, so the drama in those stories always feels overblown and out of scale. Because these stories actually belong to other people and are not taken from the lives of the politicians, I think there's a natural fear that we're being taken for chumps.

We think the stories are being used cynically and, based on experience, assume that some of the details may have been stretched for impact. Perhaps important details have been left out altogether in order to increase our empathy for the victims in the stories. Politicians are not the only ones of whom such skepticism is appropriate.

Authenticity depends on being yourself and offering lessons from your own experience. Using other people's stories is a bit like teaching math from a textbook without being able to do the math yourself. Your students and your audience will know when you're barely one chapter ahead of them in the book and they will do you the justice of not believing in you.

> *"When someone asks you, 'A penny for your thoughts,' and you put your two cents in, what happens to the other penny?" George Carlin (Comedian)*

Be careful about over-teaching your points. It's far better to make one point clearly and memorably than it is to cram the whole user manual onto an index card.

The first time I ever presented a teleclass, I got to the 45-minute mark of the one-hour session and had presented only the first third of my material. Clearly, I had started out with unreasonable expectations about how much I could cover in that hour. It was a dramatic failure of planning.

After that same teleclass, some of the feedback I received suggested that my delivery had sounded flat. I figure that came from my having been focused so much on getting through the syllabus instead of whether my audience actually learned something useful and valuable.

In the classroom, there's a real and important tension between teaching well and covering all the material in the curriculum. At root, it's a quantity versus quality debate. However, there's a legitimate argument for being able to show that anyone who has passed a course called Algebra I can do certain mathematical operations using algebra. And the teacher of Algebra II has a legitimate gripe if incoming students are unable to do those operations.

Where does this leave us? In the case of improving my teleclass, I learned that the format has its limitations so I looked for ways to get the most out of the format within its constraints. It meant that I had to focus on teaching a shorter list of fundamental principles. For those who teach in a classroom, the tension between quantity and quality never ends. I'm hopeful that the slow progress being made with the Common Core movement will help, at least, to reduce the tension.

> *"I think it's always a good move to listen to that inner voice, if it doesn't lead to a crime."* Lisa Kudrow (Actor)

You don't always know that you're about to commit a crime.

When I taught high school English, I used to give unscheduled quizzes quite often. On pop-quiz days, I got into the habit of playing classical music in my room during the passing period. Students would hear the music when they entered the room. Soon enough, they caught on to this signal and then many of the students would dive into their book to review (I hoped) or cram for the quiz (sometimes more likely).

One such quiz day, I played the "Ride of Valkyrie" by Wagner. You may remember this piece for being the background behind the famous helicopter raid scene in the movie *Apocalypse Now*. When the bell rang to start class, I quoted the movie, saying aloud, "I love the smell of napalm in the morning." It's a famous line and I thought I was being clever. But as soon as I'd said that, one of my students started to cry and ran from the room.

My stupid inner voice had forgotten that she was Cambodian and might not enjoy being reminded of images from that period of war in Southeast Asia. She returned after a short while, and after class she and I had a good talk about my error.

I learned that a truly sincere apology followed by a sincere inquiry into how I had hurt her led to an improvement in our teacher-student relationship. Admitting your mistakes and weaknesses can help put your students/audience on your side. We all make mistakes.

The relationship between teachers and their students (whether it's the adolescents in your 4th period American History class or the middle managers in your Introduction to Leadership seminar) is much like any other relationship.

As a teacher, you will be in relationship with each group that you see regularly. Each of these relationships will, in turn, work just like a one-on-one relationship. You'll grow in your ability to accept and trust each other and you'll have to work to keep it strong.

We always hear that honesty is essential to a strong relationship. That goes for the teacher/student relationship, too. Being open about your mistakes seems to strengthen relationships of all kinds. I'm sure there are smart people out there who can explain the psychology of this, but what matters to me is that it works.

Honesty really does pay.

> *"I have witnessed the softening of the hardest of hearts by a simple smile." Goldie Hawn (Actor)*

Smiles can show that you care about your students' success. And even when you're facing an audience of the most serious sorts of people, showing that you care that they get your message, showing that you care that they improve their lives or their work, and that you care about their improvement more than you care about your own success, will help get them on your side.

That's the kicker, isn't it, to care less about your own success? We live in an age that worships success to an excess. Take a quick jaunt to Amazon's immense website and do a search for books about "success" and you'll get a list with thousands of titles. There aren't enough original thinkers in the world to fill these thousands of books, and yet new books on success are published every week. Why? Because success sells these days and people seem to doubt their ability to succeed. With all this cultural pressure on us to believe that our personal and professional success matter more than almost anything else, it's easy to forget that we're working in front of an audience to ensure THEIR success, and not ours.

One of the hardest classes I ever took was an advanced French class in high school. When the teacher graded every test, he ranked each student's performance on that test and wrote it on the first page. Next to your grade would be a number representing how you stacked up against your peers on this test. I regularly placed twelfth or thirteenth out of thirteen in that class. Yet I knew for sure that the teacher, Mr. Ayotte, wanted me to do well so I wasn't discouraged.

I knew this because he always spent a few minutes chatting with me any time we ran into each other outside of class. He always had a smile for me and got me involved in related activities such as French Club. That smile and that attention mattered a great deal to me. I worked hard to do well in that class, even though the competition was fierce.

# Audience

*"Sometimes you can't see yourself clearly until you see yourself through the eyes of others." Ellen DeGeneres (Comedian and Actor)*

Knowing how your students are responding to you at any time is crucial to connecting well with them. It makes it much easier to modify your approach to ensure better comprehension, for example. But what's the best way to gauge this, to know what they're really seeing and hearing?

Their facial reactions and other responses will tell you a lot in real time. Of course there's always the trusty video camera or digital recorder to help you review your performance after the fact. Still, I don't know if there's a better way to know for sure than to get honest feedback from the audience - or a representative member of the audience - immediately afterward.

This is one of the many small points of genius in the Toastmasters educational program. In Toastmasters, there are no teachers, only peers. Every prepared speech is given a short spoken evaluation by another club member. There's nowhere to hide - you WILL get feedback on your performance. Sometimes the evaluations are presented by very experienced members and sometimes the duty falls on a newer member. Either way, the feedback is honest and almost always valuable.

Without feedback, it's really hard to learn. But feedback alone still isn't enough; it's useless if we ignore it. This is true in most endeavors, but I think the temptation to ignore feedback is particularly strong in teaching. My sense is that if our focus is mostly on our topic and not on our students, we won't have much attention available to collect and interpret feedback while we're teaching. Further, if we're overly student-focused in our work, we might let our concern for their progress block any concerns about our own learning and improvement.

To add even more obstacles, frequent feedback is not built into the system where most of us work, whether in schools, training centers, or on the speaking circuit. Some of us might collect "smile sheets" periodically, but do we really trust them?

I believe it was the Greek scientist Archimedes who said, "Give me a lever long enough and a place to stand, and I will move the world." I think that feedback is just such a lever. Give enough people honest feedback, in a spirit of cooperation and mutual respect, and you'll move the world.

It's a shame that feedback can be so hard to come by in our teaching professions. Anyone have a good fix for this?

> *"Baseball is like church. Many attend, few understand." Leo Durocher (Baseball Manager)*

Teaching is not a solo performance. Look closely at movies about strong and charismatic teachers like Jaime Escalante in *Stand and Deliver,* and you'll see the difference. Teaching is about pulling out of your students the wisdom they need to make progress in your subject. It's about turning them into disciples of your discipline.

How many times have you heard a teacher complain about the quality of students in their classes? It's not rare that this happens, is it? My own observation is that these complainers tend to be older and more experienced. In high school or college teaching, they've probably been teaching the same courses for many years. By now, all the points and concepts that usually bedevil new students seem like self-evident truths to them.

The same can happen, and does, to entrepreneurial speakers. Over time, we look for ways to vary our work and that might lead us to take short cuts through our presentations. We leave out critical steps in our train of logic. Thus, when the audience doesn't respond in the way we think they should, we blame them instead of ourselves.

The other part of my theory is that many of these complainers once imagined that they would be strong and charismatic teachers whose students would learn out of a reverence - dare I say love - for them. Instead, their students never learned very much and these teachers became more and more enamored of their own voices and stories.

In marriages, the so-called seven-year itch is real. It seems to take about seven years for a couple to work its way through the cycle from a courtship fueled by new-relationship energy (which is a potent fuel, indeed) to understanding how to truly love one another. At that point, when the excitement of the new relationship energy has dwindled, we face a sort of "Is that all there is?" question.

I wonder if the same kind of thing happens to teachers. After some period of time, our subconscious might be asking, "Is that all there is?" and it's up to us to keep the relationship with our subject alive so our students don't suffer from that point forward.

> *"There's a rule in acting called, 'Don't play the result.' If you have a character who's going to end up in a certain place, don't play that until you get there. Play each scene and each beat as it comes. And that's what you do in life: You don't play the result." Michael J. Fox (Actor)*

When adults are asked about their favorite teachers, very often the ones they mention are the science or math teachers. For some, it seems the reason for selection was "she helped me understand something that was very hard for me" and I'm sure that's often true. A good chunk of the reason might be hiding in the way that math and science are usually taught. Often they're taught by guiding students to make their own discoveries.

Even in basic geometry, we learn not just what the Pythagorean theorem is all about and how to use it, but how it was first developed. We learn to follow the right steps to discover the right answer in math problems. We learn how to do experiments in chemistry lab and how to learn anatomy through dissection in biology. Good learning is about discovery and you won't know the answer until it's actually in front of you on your math homework or the lab tray.

What does it look like when we play the result, as Michael J. Fox put it? I think this is the teacher who talks in platitudes. These are the teachers whose stories all have happy endings that show only the successful decisions in a life that surely contained plenty of failures. It's the teacher who never checks in with the audience to see how well they're getting it. It's the teacher who has memorized the PowerPoint bullet points but no longer bothers to explain the logical progression that they summarize.

It's the almost-inevitable consequence of boiling a half-day workshop down to a 45-minute lecture just because that's what the client wants. Now to be fair, most teachers don't fall into this trap. But it's a deep one and I can imagine that it might be hard to find your way out when you do fall in.

This is also why so many of the very best teachers show a kind of youthful enthusiasm for their work, even as they approach the end of their careers. If you start ever class not at all certain how it will end, the inevitable curiosity and suspense are bound to feed your work in good ways.

*"Find somebody to be successful for. Raise their hopes. Think of their needs." Barack Obama (U.S. President)*

I read many newsletters and blog posts aimed at helping solo entrepreneurs improve their businesses. A very common recommendation I see is this: in order to sell your services you need to show potential customers how you can help them. What pain can you ease with your unique blend of personality, expertise, and service? It's not always easy to answer this question, by the way. I suspect this difficulty is a large part of why so many entrepreneurial ventures fail in their first few years.

The same advice holds in the classroom and the meeting room: what specific solution can you provide to help this particular group of people solve their unique problems? Every year's Algebra II class is a little different from the previous year's group. Every Rotary Club meeting audience is a little bit different, and the members of that club are certainly different from a group of Fortune 500 company presidents. To know their unique set of needs first and then build your teaching around their needs seems to be the right way to go.

Now, to be fair, there's also the opposing argument to consider: that you can never really know your audience well enough to prepare for every personality you'll face. Still, I think that you can learn enough to make a difference.

# Delivery

> *"Think like a wise man but communicate in the language of the people." William Butler Yeats (Poet)*

If I'm a student or I'm in a speaker's audience, all I really care about is me. What can I learn, how do I get an A, or what can I pick up from this speech that will help my business? I may be sitting in a group of several hundred, but I'm only one person. I don't want to hear the teacher talk to the group as if we're a cohesive whole who have only one mind and one reason for being in the room. I want the teacher to be talking only to me.

Most times, I could hardly care less if my neighbor gets anything out of the class or presentation. A teacher might ask, "How many of you have had this experience?" and I'm tempted to turn off my attention. He's not talking only to me and that makes me think that he might not care about my unique needs. That's how I react and I doubt that I'm alone in responding this way.

Instead, if the teacher says, "Has this ever happened to you?" or "How many times have you done this?" then I'm listening intently. I hear "you" and now I'm sure that he's talking directly to me. Now we've begun a one-on-one teaching and learning session no matter how many others are in the room. That's why I walked into the room in the first place.

Several months ago, I gave a talk to a group of Toastmasters. I told them how my life has improved from participating in Toastmasters. I opened the speech this way: "They say that laughter is good medicine." When I was asked to repeat the speech several weeks later, I changed that opening to this: "How many of us have faced a challenge and felt that it might be too much to handle?" To be candid, neither opening worked very well.

A few months after that, I attended a workshop led by Patricia Fripp, one of the finest speaking coaches in the business. One of the lessons she taught us was that using the word "you" by itself in the place of "how many of you" and similar constructions helps a teacher make a direct, one-on-one connection with the audience members. When I was asked to give that same speech a third time, I changed my opening to, "How often have you felt that you didn't quite have what it takes to meet the challenges of your day?" It's still not quite perfect and I'm sure I could condense it a bit more, but as soon as I started the speech this way, every face in the audience told me that we were already connecting.

That was a breakthrough moment for me.

## *"Never fight an inanimate object."*
## *P. J. O'Rourke (Journalist)*

Hell hath no fury like a laptop scorned. Or something like that. Imagine that you're dressed in your best suit and you have precisely seven minutes to prove that you are the best presenter among a group of several. Is your first instinct to fire up a laptop and wow the audience with your PowerPoint skills? I didn't think so.

That should tell you everything you need to know about presentation software like PowerPoint. It's. Not. Really. Necessary. Helpful, sure, but not at all necessary. Using projected slides complicates everything about speaking and teaching except, maybe, the use of handouts.

Now, we all know there are times when projecting slides can help you put useful information in front of your audience in a hurry. In fact, recently I heard a talk that would have been improved with a couple of slides. But when was the last time you saw a presentation with only two slides? I thought so.

When you're a solo consultant, you find yourself studying what other consultants say about how they became successful. You soak up their lessons to avoid making the mistakes they say held them back. One of my consultant-heroes is David Maister. David retired recently, but he was the consummate solo teacher. And he NEVER used PowerPoint. He used a flipchart or a white board. He said that he never wanted to be constrained by a pre-set structure in his presentations, preferring instead to facilitate discussions. Learning, in his view, worked best when it was collaborative and organic. That is, learning is most effective when the group finds its own path to discovery.

We should be paying attention to this lesson.

> *"There's no present. There's only the immediate future and the recent past." George Carlin (Comedian)*

As I learned from comedian and actor Stephen Fry, it's impossible to do nothing. Those students or audience members who look like they're zoned out and aren't doing anything while you teach? They're not doing nothing.

They might be thinking about the next time they'll have sex or what they're going to have for dinner tonight. Or, they might be thinking about something you said a minute ago. They're probably responding to your teaching, but because they're processing what you told them a moment ago, they're most likely falling behind you at any time during your presentation. What can you do about this lag?

We all process new information a little differently. This is the fundamental principle of the learning styles theory, after all. And at least that much of the theory is true. Some of us need more time to process verbal inputs than visual ones, or we need some tinkering hands-on time to make new information sink in most efficiently. Underlying the

34

fact of the differences is this even more fundamental fact - we all need time to process and store new information, regardless of how we receive it.

I talk fast, sometimes too fast, especially when I'm excited or passionate about my topic. I need to remind myself regularly to just shut up. Let them think, John. Let them think.

Silence. I recommend silence.

> *"I may not have gone where I intended to go, but I think I have ended up where I needed to be." Douglas Adams (Science Fiction Writer)*

One of my favorite teaching tools is the discussion. Given a finite amount of time, such as the typical 45 minutes of a high school English class or the one hour of a speaking gig, the tension between letting a discussion lead wherever it may go and the need to reach a predetermined destination so that the learners get the main point of the lesson is tantalizing. It's like a drug that both tempts you and feeds you. The best part of taking this drug is that along the way, it's almost a given that a good discussion will yield ideas that you never could have planned on.

For example, ask a set of people to talk about the failure of The American Dream and you might end up with insights into how successful people plan their successes and others don't. Even though you never imagined that the discussion might go in that direction. Discussions are a bit like wandering through a great department store or antiques shop. You never know what kind of treasure you will find in the next aisle.

Sometimes in leading a discussion you do have to stop for some cleanup in aisle three. You find yourself on a detour that just won't ever get you to where you need to go. A detour that might take you on more tangents than you've seen since Geometry I. These detours call for some re-direction.

Then we have to ask: how can you tell the difference between a detour that can only take you to a washed out bridge and one that will lead to new and valuable insights? It would be easy to say that you'll know one when you see one. But that's not fair, is it?

The answer is that you have to know two things to recognize the useful detours. First, you have to know your subject well enough to know most of the good insights that a group might generate. That takes study, planning, and experience in working with the subject. Second, it helps to know the common misconceptions that people might share about your subject. Knowing where the pitfalls are, what the errors in thinking are, will help you lead your audience away from them as you go.

In the end, while leading discussions can appear at first to be easier than lecturing, it's quite possible that the reverse is true.

*"I know that you believe that you understood what you think I said, but I am not sure you realize that what you heard is not what I meant." Robert McCloskey (Young Adult Author)*

How often do you find yourself teaching as if what you were doing was largely a performance? Lecturing, for example, instead of leading a discussion? One danger, and it's a big one, in thinking of teaching or speaking as a performance, is that we lose out on being able to easily identify whether our audience is getting it as we speak. Clarity of expression is important, and so is comprehension.

While it's true that communication goes two ways, I hold that the speaker has the greater responsibility. She must be sure that what she wanted to communicate was actually received by the listener. While it may seem daunting to turn a keynote address to a few thousand people into a conversation, it's not impossible. It doesn't take a great deal of conversation with an audience member to check on comprehension, but it's worth the effort.

What good is it to speak for an hour or lecture on Newton's Third Law, if you walk away from the session unsure that your message was received? Why bother to start, in that case?

I suppose what we're really talking about here is responsibility. Who holds the responsibility in the act of teaching? Plenty of people will tell you that most of the responsibility falls on the teacher. Others might put a larger share of responsibility on the student. To some extent, they're both right. But for both to be right, we'd have to give up the idea that teaching is a kind of performance, wouldn't we?

Because if we hold that the student has the majority of the responsibility - or even just some of the responsibility - doesn't that mean that we expect the student to act on her own behalf? That she can't merely be a passive observer of our performance? And if she has to be active, doesn't that mean that instead of being performers, we should be facilitators? I thought so. It's a shared responsibility but we, as teachers, have to set the process in motion.

*"It is difficult to produce a television documentary that is both incisive and probing when every twelve minutes one is interrupted by twelve dancing rabbits singing about toilet paper." Rod Serling (Television Writer)*

---

You can't turn a good presentation into a great one with a single sentence, but you can certainly turn a good presentation into a bad one with a single phrase. Such phrases as "at the end of the day" or "needless to say" can destroy a good presentation in moments. When I hear teachers use such phrases, I start to wonder if the quality of their thinking is as sloppy as their language. Such phrases are worse than clichés because they convey even less information than a cliché. They waste my time and give me the impression that the teacher hasn't done the work to achieve real clarity about his lesson.

I have a friend who coaches professionals in business to boost their confidence. He says that confidence cures many problems with decision-making. In the same way, clarity of thinking cures many problems for teachers. When you know precisely what lesson you intend to teach and have strong supporting evidence, many of the mechanical issues of preparing the presentation will take care of themselves. Not sure what your PowerPoint slides should say? Being able to state your lesson in one clear sentence with a few equally clear supporting sentences will give you the structure and language of your slides.

Not sure about what stories to include? Clarity about your supporting points should help you pick just the right stories from your experience. You'll easily channel Abraham Lincoln, who often began to speak with these words, "That reminds me of a story."

So...in 25 words or less, what are you teaching? And what do you provide as supporting evidence to demonstrate the truth of your lesson? Also in 25 words or less, of course.

## *"Memory feeds imagination." Amy Tan (Novelist)*

Sometimes I try to imagine the scene when something innovative happened for the first time. What must it have been like to get the idea to cook animal flesh for the first time? What was it like to taste such cooked meat for the first time. What did it feel like to learn of exotic places from a traveling story-teller when you'd never ventured more than a few miles from your primitive village back in the Iron Age? We may have lost the sense of wonder at learning new things, perhaps in part because of the Internet. It's so easy to find the answer to any question. It takes a powerful story to teach the children of the Internet.

I learned an important story-telling lesson from Mikki Williams, who is one of my favorite Chicago-area speakers. She made this point when teaching a class for the National Speakers Association here:

when you're telling a story from your own experience, do your best to relive the emotions that you felt at the time. This will make the telling much more believable and thus more moving.

Mikki's own signature story involves a handkerchief and tears that she shed with her mother late in her mother's life. When she concludes this story, she always pulls a handkerchief from a pocket and the tears - real tears - start to fall. You can't miss her emotion and, as a result, the story personalizes her lesson for the audience. Then, when she points out that she's using the same handkerchief that she had used at her mother's hospital bed, she puts tears in everyone else's eyes. That, my friends, is story-telling by a pro.

My wife often tells of an embarrassing moment that happened when she was living in France. First, some necessary background: the French language uses different words for "you" depending on the level of formality between the speakers. Friends use one form and unacquainted people use the more formal form. Thus, one would use the formal "you" when speaking with a civic official like a judge when you're conducting official business.

Now, let's get back to my wife's story. It was a presidential election year in the U.S. (no, I'm not foolish enough to reveal the year) and she needed to have her absentee ballot notarized by a local judge. Karen slipped and used the informal form of "you" when she thanked the judge for his assistance with the ballot. He shrugged it off, as she tells the story, but no doubt he was thinking, "Stupid

American," complete with that huffy accent you hear in bad movies.

When she tells this story in class, it's very effective. Even though it has been several years since the incident, she still feels a bit of the embarrassment. Her students pick up on the embarrassment and thus the lesson of the grammatical point is made a little more memorable.

Stories turn presenters into teachers.

# Growth

*"The strongest principle of growth lies in human choice." George Eliot (Novelist)*

There is an old joke about psychiatry: how many psychiatrists does it take to change a light bulb? The answer: only one, but the light bulb must want to change. Desire to change has to exist before change can happen. It seems that learning works the same way. When you sit in an audience to hear a teacher, don't you find yourself choosing whether to buy her argument, to agree with her points? Don't you find yourself judging her presentation, deciding whether she was truly persuasive?

Learning happens by choice.

When our son Matt was born, I took the gig as stay-at-home Dad for his first year. Like any infant, Matt slept for hours every day and I found myself looking for things to do. I decided to try my hand at making a few simple Christmas gifts from wood. I had been a terrible student in junior high school shop class, so I had a lot to learn before I could make those gifts. I chose to learn how to make strong and attractive joints and all the other skills I needed. I found that choosing to learn made it much easier to learn these skills as an adult than it had been as a young teenager.

Because I had chosen to gain these new skills, my motivation was high and it was easier to persist through struggles. There's a reason for the woodworker's commandment: "Measure twice, cut once." It's really frustrating to make an irrevocable mistake. When you take time to carefully prepare a board to be a table leg, for example, and then you let a tool slip and gouge the leg beyond repair at the last minute, you've wasted hours of work. You might even have to buy more wood to replace the ruined piece. If this happens often, as it usually does to a beginner, it can take real will power to persevere.

Second, I paid close attention to my learning, which shortened the learning curve. That, too, came from choosing to learn. Being intentional about learning opens us up to the feedback we get. Because we want to learn, we're more open to negative feedback, to seeing our errors and slip-ups. The desire helps us take the punches from those slip-ups and gives us the will to learn from them. It's in the choosing that we begin to learn.

*"The moment of victory is much too short to live for that and nothing else." Martina Navratilova (Tennis Player)*

When I was taking classes through the National Speakers Association, the most difficult moments for me came when our instructors would insist that we identify that one thing inside of us that's burning to get out. I was never quite sure what my one burning thing was, and that's both embarrassing and depressing. But if we don't have a burning desire to help people, why do we teach?

What gifts we have, we should want to share with others, don't you think? At least that's what I see in the teachers that I know and admire. For some, it's the joy of accomplishment and they do marvelous jobs entertaining and motivating their audiences. For others, it's the gift of making the sale and understanding how to get to "yes." They are inspiring sales trainers. Others still are lovers of science or literature or language. They share these gifts as naturally as a youngster might share a bag of popcorn.

What I've learned about myself is that my expertise is in me. It's in what I have done with my professional life, a combination of teaching and training and speaking. And writing, which is why I chose to write this little book.

Why do we need to have a burning desire to teach our one true thing? Teaching is hard work. We put our egos on the line every time we step in front of the room. We test our minds to simultaneously communicate our lesson and gauge how well the audience is getting it. We stress our voices and our bodies when we teach for long stretches of time.

It's hard, self-sacrificing work and the pay, let's face it, isn't always what we'd like. So yes, having that burning desire to teach, to be liked, to give of yourself, makes it so much easier to stand up and share yourself in all your glory and warts.

The applause is great. Seeing your students succeed is satisfying, and knowing that your learners will do good work on the job is an enduring pleasure. But make no mistake: what we do is hard and it would be terrifyingly more difficult if we didn't wake up every morning with a desire that was stronger than the challenge.

> *"This became a credo of mine...attempt the impossible in order to improve your work." Bette Davis (Actor)*

As someone once said, it's better to have loved and lost than never to have loved at all. One of my favorite parts of Toastmasters is the semi-annual speech contests. Each year, members of Toastmasters clubs compete in four different contests, each one calling on a different set of skills. The contests begin with each club choosing a champion and then all those club champions compete against one another in several levels of elimination contests until a champion is crowned.

In a speech contest you can't play defense against your opponent. All you can do is to execute your very best performance. You have to figure out what's your best. And then make it happen.

Those who win these contests earn the respect and admiration of their peers and I can say from experience that I never work quite so hard to improve a presentation as I do when I compete in these contests. The speeches must fit into a prescribed set of time limits, so every word, every gesture must pull its weight. The effort to be the best, to improve one's game to the level needed to win, made me a better speaker and, for that matter, a better writer.

To be blunt, we should prepare every lesson and every speech as carefully as this. Every lesson should be as tightly constructed as an essay worthy of being published in the *New Yorker* magazine. We rarely take time to do this, and for classroom teachers it would be a ludicrously high expectation. Still, we all have certain key lessons that we teach repeatedly and these core lessons deserve our best thinking and writing.

> *"It's all right letting yourself go as long as you can let yourself back."*
> *Mick Jagger (Rock Musician)*

Let's say that you've decided to improve your presentation so you record it. Now it's time to watch or listen to your work. How do you learn from this? What do you look for? When do you know that you've done enough analysis and can start working on specific improvements?

Darren LaCroix, a former Toastmasters World Champion of Public Speaking shows a picture of all the video tapes he has made of his own presentations when he presents on the subject of improving your speaking skills. The photo shows dozens, probably hundreds, of tapes. He has studied every one of them.

To make his point, Darren likes to say, "Everyone wants to have my trophy, but no one wants my closet [full of video tapes]." He's right. Most of us don't want to push ourselves that hard.

It's popular these days to claim that you need 10,000 hours of practice to become an expert. I don't think this is quite right. You need many hours of intentional, systematic and debriefed practice to perform at an expert level. The number may vary from one person to the next. Being intentional and systematic and debriefing yourself is the constant.

How about spending just one hour studying a tape of your work? As you watch or listen, make these lists for yourself:

- Three things I did very well.
- Four things that I didn't like.
- Five things the audience liked

Now, pick one of the items in the middle list to eliminate first. Then get rid of it in your next presentation. You'll know if you succeeded by watching the tape of that next performance.

> *"I can't give you a sure-fire formula for success, but I can give you a formula for failure: try to please everybody all the time." Herbert Bayard Swope (Journalist)*

Do you remember seeing actress Sally Field's acceptance speech when she won the Oscar for her work in the movie *Places in the Heart*? That was when she said "I haven't had an orthodox career. And I've wanted more than anything to have your respect. The first time I didn't feel it. But this time I feel it. And I can't deny the fact that you like me... right now ...you like me. Thank you." Clearly she had a powerful drive to be liked and admired by her peers, her fellow actors. I think that many of us teach from similar motives, at least in part.

As youngsters, we got our teachers to like us by raising our hands often with the right answers in class. We studied hard so we'd earn their approval - and high grades - at test time. We still have that need to be liked now that it's our turn at the front of the room. We soften the edges of our material or we shy away from dramatic expressions. We try to impress everyone, maybe with complex arguments or by name dropping. We tell jokes more to build rapport than to advance our lessons. And in the process, we drift a bit too far from the core lessons we want to teach.

Recently I attended a presentation given by a teacher with many decades of experience. He told us about a time when he was advised to make his class more interactive and "student-friendly." He told us he replied, "I'd like to but when I ask my students to explain the differences between abstract and concrete language, they get it wrong and I just have to teach it anyway." In truth, some of his class sessions are quite interactive but his lectures really are old-fashioned lectures filled with clearly presented information and that he makes lively with entertaining and pertinent stories. In the nearly four-hour presentation that I attended, he only softened the dialog of a few of his stories and never softened his message. The stories that he modified weren't entirely "family friendly," if you know what I mean.

Honesty and truth, even when difficult, should be easy to spot in our lessons.

> *"We are told that talent creates its own opportunities. But it sometimes seems that intense desire creates not only its own opportunities, but its own talents." Eric Hoffer (Philosopher)*

They say that if you work hard enough and want something badly enough, you can get it. Really? I'm skeptical and I believe this idea is rooted in a falsehood. That falsehood ignores the fact that simple luck plays a large part in success. After all, in most of the Horatio Alger stories, the plucky young hero often gets ahead only after he catches the eye of a prominent benefactor or mentor, and if that's not luck then I'm not sure what luck looks like.

Let's consider the possibility, not at all uncommon, that you have lost a job and want a new way to make a living. This is going to mean acquiring new skills. I have many friends who have moved from sales or various corporate roles into professional coaching. Now, instead of meeting the goals of an employer, they're self-employed coaches who help others to achieve their goals. To do this, they've had to reorganize their skills and build new ones.

How might it work, exactly, for desire to create its own talents? I wonder: what does intense desire cause us to do that will lead to new talents? One product of desire is the capacity to push oneself harder than normal to meet challenging goals. Another is a willingness to pay close attention to our own efforts.

I know this was the case when I was teaching myself woodworking. I was constantly faced with challenges I hadn't ever encountered before and that I couldn't meet without learning some new technique or how to use a new tool. Sometimes I had to hone a skill that wasn't quite strong enough.

What does this mean for teachers? I think that this tension created by intense desire might be one of the secrets of charismatic teachers. They inspire in their students a desire to please them and receive their praise and this desire may be strong enough to inspire new talents. But if I think that I'm not a charismatic person, how can I harness this capacity of desire? There's hope, for if we teach authentically and let our passion for our subject show through, that passion will be the source of our own charisma.

> *"A single day is enough to make us a little larger." Paul Klee (Painter)*

It's important to remember that insightful breakthroughs don't happen on a schedule. You won't find them on your calendar, no matter how hard you look. Instead, think of the merits of regular, consistent effort.

Let's say you set out to write a novel. Even a short novel is at least 50,000 words long. For those who take on the challenge, National Novel Writing Month (affectionately known among writers as NaNoWriMo) is about writing a 50,000 word novel in one month (usually November). To produce 50,000 words in one month you must write about 1,667 words every day. Aim for those 1,667 words for a few days and you may find, as some of my writer friends have, that some days you will crank out as many as 5,000 words. That level of production makes the novel go faster, of course, but it can also make for easier writing on the days when you slow down to the steadier pace.

There's a catch, though (there always is, right?). You won't ever find yourself belting out words at a 5,000-per-day pace if you aren't writing every day to begin with.

Regular consistent effort is the world-sized lever that gives power to the large, single goal. Philosophers of success claim that the best secret to success is to keep in your mind a single large goal. We learned this from Napoleon Hill in his book *Think and Grow Rich* and I'm sure he got the idea from someone before him. What makes this work - at least much of the time - is that the path to a single large goal is a long one and we can only get there in small steps. One day, one week, one milestone at a time.

# Humor

> *"If you watch a game, it's fun. If you play at it, it's recreation. If you work at it, it's golf." Bob Hope (Comedian)*

I play golf. Well, to be fair, I play at golf. My golf swing looks like I'm trying to kill a snake while wearing a blindfold, but still I like golf. I like the thinking that's required and I like that an old guy like me can still play a sport.

This Bob Hope joke reminds me that humor often works in a three-beat pattern. The power of many jokes is that the punch line arrives in the third instance in a series. To illustrate this pattern, here's a joke I made up for the occasion. "I think I've found the perfect guy for me. He's taller than me, quite handsome, and he didn't change his phone number after our first date." Yes, I know you've heard many jokes that were much funnier but this one isn't terrible, it shows my point, and it's good evidence that Jerry Seinfeld won't be hiring me to write comedy for his next hit sitcom.

I find it hard, though, to discipline myself to use this kind of three-beat humor. Sometimes I am more like Jeff Foxworthy as he repeats his "You might be a redneck" routine formula ("If you go to family reunions to pick up women, you might be a redneck. If your belt buckle is bigger than your head, you might be a redneck."). Much of the humor in Foxworthy's routine comes from the specific examples, of course, but the power in this routine comes from the sheer volume of observations. Like Foxworthy, I often tend to go for quantity over quality.

In teaching, we should probably stick with shorter and punchier humor, sprinkling it in our work like a strong spice. I suppose it's not a good thing for a teacher to be confused with a comedian, though I think I'm not at risk for that.

We can learn from the Bob Hopes of the world.

> *"The wit makes fun of other persons; the satirist makes fun of the world; the humorist makes fun of himself." James Thurber (Humorist)*

Endeavor to be a humorist and make yourself the butt of your jokes. You can tell jokes about other people all day long but in the end they always sound a bit mean spirited (This is the heart of all those terrible ethnic jokes like "three Irishmen walk into a bar..."). And you almost always insult someone in the audience when you do this. Instead, make yourself the butt of your jokes and let them laugh at you.

What's the old saying? "Laugh and the world laughs with you, weep, and you weep alone." Actually, this is not an old saying for it comes from a poem called "Solitude" by Ella Wheeler Wilcox that was published in 1918. I haven't read the whole poem, but these lines speak to the very human preference for sharing in others' joy and avoiding their pain.

There are exceptions: when that pain comes from being hit on the head by your friend Moe when your name is Larry or Curly. Or when you stumble and fall while wearing a tuxedo and your name is Cary Grant. People remember Cary Grant for being suave and handsome, which he was, but they forget the millions of laughs he got for falling down, looking ridiculous, or being upstaged by a dog.

We loved to laugh at Cary Grant when he was baffled by Katherine Hepburn in all those movies they did together. Every time we laughed, it was because Cary was the butt of the joke, and not because he'd made someone else look foolish.

I could handle being a little more like Cary Grant., couldn't you?

> *"Students achieving Oneness will move on to Twoness." Woody Allen (Movie Director)*

People learn things best one principle or task at a time. When you plan a training program around this principle, you're using what many people call "chunking." But there's a problem with chunking.

It's really hard to apply the chunking principle in its strictest form in real-life teaching. Motivational speakers seem to be guided by the belief that they must teach their lessons in groups of 3, 4, or 5 and have a snappy acronym for their audience to remember them by. This is clearly what their audiences have come to expect and what they demand. Straying from this pattern to chunk the lessons in a keynote seems like it would be financial suicide.

If you're teaching Geometry I, you can proceed one theorem at a time for a while, but even most of the basic theorems involve more than one principle. And don't even begin to think about how to use the chunking method to teach the novel *Huckleberry Finn*. That dog won't hunt, as they say.

Instead, it makes sense to think in terms of teaching recursively using small chunk-like building blocks. In recursive teaching, we introduce a principle at its simplest level at one time and then return to it repeatedly, adding complexity with each visit. My children began to work on math problems involving algebra in elementary school when they had barely learned to multiply. Over the course of two or three years, their teachers introduced more and more fundamentals of algebra in short bursts. In the end, they were using algebra two or three years earlier than my wife and I had when we were forced to learn it all at once.

I wonder what it would look like to try this recursive method in a self-contained one-hour presentation like a keynote address. Maybe we could introduce an idea at its most basic level and then return to it several times, each time treating it on a higher level of thinking. To do this, we could follow the levels of Bloom's Taxonomy. It might be a fascinating experience for everyone involved, including the speaker.

To begin at the Knowledge level, we would state our thesis and define its terms with specific facts or data. Then we move up to the Comprehension level by amplifying our thesis with graphs. Moving up to the Application level, we could show how our thesis works in the real world, perhaps by showing how someone might profit by applying our idea in a challenging business situation.

At the Analysis level and show how various well-known persons either failed or succeeded according to our principle. At the Synthesis level - nearly to the top now - we demonstrate how our principle would work together with other principles to create better outcomes. Finally, at the Evaluation level, we could tell a story and challenge our students to evaluate the characters' actions according to the principle we're teaching.

Thus we'd have engaged our audience with one principle in ever-more challenging levels of thinking. We've circled back to our principle repeatedly, but from different angles. My guess is that if we did this, the audience would know our principle cold. I think this could work. Sometimes a corkscrew is the shortest path to something good besides a glass of cabernet sauvignon.

*"There are two kinds of people in the world, those who believe there are two kinds of people in the world and those who don't." Robert Benchley (Journalist)*

Another way to put this: there are 10 types of people in the world: those who understand binary and those who don't.

In the three teaching worlds where I have worked, it seems that teachers come in two varieties: those who identify as subject matter experts and those who identify as teacher/facilitators. The strengths and insecurities of these two groups are complementary.

I have always tended to teach in facilitator mode.

Leading discussions plays to my strengths. I'm not truly happy as a teacher unless the class is so deeply engaged in our discussion that we are in danger of working well past our allotted time.

At the same time, I admire anyone whose knowledge of their subject is encyclopedic and who does a good job of inspiring students to learn. Still, I used to look down on the subject-matter expert types because, in my view, they weren't really teaching. I wondered if maybe they presented that way because they didn't have strong people skills, or at least couldn't use them very well. So I saw those teachers as being somehow defective, or intruders who took up a teaching slot that belonged to a REAL teacher.

Then I studied under Al Davis. The Linguistics department chair at Illinois Institute of Technology, Al knew more about linguistics than anyone I had met before or since. He often lectured for two or three hours without notes and presented a completely cogent explanation of how the dialects of American English developed, for example. Then, without seeming to change personalities at all, he would turn Socratic and drag each of his graduate students to a deeper understanding of the topic at hand. The man knew how to frame questions to elicit the answers we needed to construct.

It's possible to be both a subject-matter expert and a great facilitator. But such people are rare.

# Truth

*"No man is so foolish but he may sometimes give another good counsel, and no man so wise that he may not easily err if he takes no other counsel than his own. He that is taught only by himself has a fool for a master." Hunter S. Thompson (Journalist)*

Learn from the greats, but don't ever pass up the feedback of an amateur. DaVinci and Michelangelo copied the works of great artists who came before them when they were learning their craft. Why? They copied to develop their own skills, to learn the masters' secrets, and then to try to surpass their masters. This is a model for skill development that has largely disappeared from our modern experience.

Writing clear sentences is not easy and not all students pick up the skill of writing clearly from the beginning. As a high school English teacher in summer school, I worked with students who had failed English. It wasn't a class of prospective Rhodes Scholars in other words. One of their real weaknesses, almost universally, was an inability to write clearly.

We didn't have time in a crowded summer-school schedule to include much in-class writing work and these students weren't the most reliable about doing homework. But - and this is important - they mostly needed to pass my class to get their high school diploma. Enter motivation, stage left.

As an experiment, I offered these students an extra credit option. Any students who would buy a notebook and fill it with pages copied from good magazines like *Time*, *Newsweek*, or *Sports Illustrated* would receive extra credit. Several took me up on the idea, and in just a few weeks they started writing more clearly. They started making stronger arguments by using better examples to back up their points. Their syntax and spelling improved and I saw fewer and fewer sentences that confused the issue rather than illuminating it.

Seeing how better writers did their work helped them improve their own writing.

My point is not to glorify some teaching technique that I tried with some success twenty years ago. Instead, it's to remind myself that students can often teach themselves with just a little guidance.

*"When you make the finding yourself - even if you're the last person on Earth to see the light - you'll never forget it." Carl Sagan (Astrophysicist)*

Discovery, or being in charge of one's own learning, is the very heart of science. And what is science, after all, but well-organized learning? We should all be scientists of learning and encourage our students to do the same.

When I was very young, I wanted to be a scientist when I grew up. In fact, I held onto this surely impossible dream right up until my freshman year in high school.

I also wanted to be an astronaut, inspired by the early flights in the American space program. Alan Shepard, John Glenn, and Jim Lovell—the astronauts who flew the Mercury, Gemini and Apollo missions—became my heroes. In my view, they were very specialized scientists, so dreaming of space flight was connected to my hope of becoming a scientist.

During my freshman year in high school, my dream to become a scientist changed. Well, evaporated is more accurate. It was boiled out of me and became a dream to become a writer. I came to the conclusion that writing was for me because writers wouldn't have to use algebra, which was clearly some kind of dark art. If I learned anything in Mrs. Ellis's Algebra I class, it was that I would surely starve if I had to rely on algebra to make a living.

Eventually I settled on teaching for my career and, at some point, I even learned how to do algebra. What never left me was the desire to do what scientists do: learn new things in a very intentional way. Through observation or experimentation, science is all about intentionally learning one new thing at a time and how that new bit of knowledge either fits our understanding of the world or shakes it up.

This early desire - the dream of one day becoming a space-travelling Pasteur or Galileo - was the foundation for my personal philosophy of teaching. We experience one new thing at a time, and we learn from it by reflecting on how it changes our understanding of the world. A teacher's job is to make this happen.

Which leads me to ask this: what's the core of your teaching philosophy?

> *"The truth does not change according to our ability to stomach it." Flannery O'Connor (Novelist)*

One of my most embarrassing moments came at the very beginning of my teaching career. After graduating from college, I joined a group called The Teacher Corps. We were kissing cousins with the Peace Corps (hey, it was the early seventies, after all) and I was assigned to work in a Teacher Corps team at a junior high school in a poor section of Lackawanna, New York. On the outskirts of Buffalo, our school was practically in the shadow of the largest steel mill run by Bethlehem Steel at the time.

One of our first learning experiences in Teacher Corps was to present a short lesson to our peers that would be videotaped. Over the course of the year, several of our lessons were videotaped like that and then we reviewed the tapes for feedback. But that first taped lesson is the one that sticks in my memory. When I finished watching the tape with our cooperating teacher and the rest of my team, I wanted to resign and drive back home to Maine. I. Was. Terrible. Awful. On that tape, I looked like a terribly arrogant, pedantic so-and-so who had no business teaching seventh graders.

The feedback I got from watching that tape of my first prepared lesson was absolutely essential to my development as a teacher. But here's the more important lesson: getting feedback is completely useless if we don't take the time to reflect on it and find ways to improve our performance.

It's in the post-feedback reflection that we ponder how to avoid such big mistakes. From that video, I became aware of a small multitude of odd physical movements and twitches that I should eliminate. I learned it was ludicrous to have spent time writing a lesson on how to teach seventh graders about the twelve layers of symbolism in *Ulysses* by James Joyce. Beyond that, I didn't interact with my "students" even once. I had gone into that exercise quite sure that I was a naturally gifted teacher and I came out knowing that I was going to have to work hard to become merely adequate.

I had a lot to learn, but the learning began with those first moments of reflecting on whether it would be wise to just walk out the door. I'm glad I didn't.

*"The truth is the kindest thing we can give folks in the end." Harriet Beecher Stowe (Novelist)*

In youth sports these days, everyone gets a trophy. Call me old-fashioned if you like, but I think that does the kids a disservice. I'm all in favor of giving kids a memento at the end of a sports season. But where I part ways with the trophy-givers is this: a trophy should be about unusual accomplishment, even superiority. So when we give every kid on the soccer team a trophy just for showing up (even though Woody Allen says that 80% of success is showing up), we're giving them the wrong feedback.

Imagine the process of learning to putt a golf ball. The two key skills in putting are to hit the ball in the right direction and with the right amount of force. Done right, the ball will roll directly toward the hole without going past it or stopping short. With easily demonstrated learning objectives like these, the teaching (and learning) should be pretty straightforward, don't you think?

Now try to imagine learning to putt blindfolded. You'd need someone to help you line up the ball in front of your club. Your teacher would also have to tell you what happened each time you putted a ball. Did the ball go left or right of the hole? Did it stop short or go past the hole? Without this feedback, you'd never know how to adjust your putting stroke to make it more accurate. But with a coach who gave you accurate feedback after every try, eventually you'd be able to putt fairly well, even with a blindfold.

Now try to imagine this same learning exercise - putting while blindfolded - with a different coach. This new coach watches you putt and after every try he says, "Great job" but gives no other feedback. I'm sure you see the problem here. With feedback like that, you'd never learn to putt.

Feedback matters, but accurate feedback matters even more.

> *"We have, as human beings, a storytelling problem. We're a bit too quick to come up with explanations for things we don't really have an explanation for." Malcolm Gladwell (Writer)*

Beware the easy answer, the simple formula, the trite advice. It's so easy to think that we can teach others based on a quick reading of someone else's work. For example, when I first started work as a training consultant, Stephen Covey's book *The 7 Habits of Highly Effective People* was relatively new and was extremely popular. It seemed as if nearly every corporate trainer I met in those early days had put together some small piece of training based on one of the principles or ideas in Covey's 7 Habits book.

I sat through a few of these sessions and they were, almost all of them, quite wretched. The ideas were presented without context or were very poorly explained, and more often than not the participants learned very little. More than that, the participants grew to distrust the trainer, which would have negatively affected all future training by that trainer.

Two things caused the problems in those training lessons. The trainer didn't have the time to present all of the context present in Covey's book. When we skip - or badly abbreviate - the context while teaching a new principle, the end result is usually bad. And what's often woven into that context is the essential element of "what's in it for me" that most learners need. Without a reason to learn, and without a reason to trust the teacher, few people will learn very much.

Also, some of those trainers didn't really understand Covey's principles and presented weak interpretations of them that widely missed the point. I suspect that some of them had never read the book at all. Sitting in those sessions was a bit like drinking coffee made from grounds that had been used at least once before.

This might seem to be condescending, but we do our students no good when we don't fully understand our material or give it short shrift. Remember the game Telephone, where a simple message becomes garbled after it's repeated several times by a long line of people? That last person shouldn't be the one to take responsibility for teaching the original message.

*"They say such nice things about people at their funerals that it makes me sad to realize that I'm going to miss mine by just a few days." Garrison Keillor (Radio Show Host)*

One can divide teachers in many different ways, but one that makes a lot of sense is to divide them by how they interact with students. One group of teachers likes to play the expert and bully. Remember the movie *The Paper Chase*, starring John Houseman as much-feared law professor Charles Kingfield? You may remember Houseman better for his appearances in commercials for the Smith Barney brokerage firm ("We make money the old fashioned way - we *earn* it.").

In the movie, Kingfield's law-school class sessions are minefields of abuse and scorn for any student who answers questions poorly. And they nearly all answered questions poorly in Kingfield's opinion. He was the prototypical expert-bully.

Now think of the movie *Stand and Deliver*, starring Edward James Olmos as teacher Jaime Escalante. In this movie, Escalante constantly urges his students to exceed their own expectations, frequently praising their smallest improvements. Escalante, who was a real teacher with remarkable success teaching Advanced Placement Math in the inner city, was the prototypical teacher-coach.

If we take seriously that education means to draw out of our students, then the teacher-coach is the one who draws out the best in her students and the expert-bully is the one who forces the students to find their own best and reveal it through a fight. Both approaches can work. Which type are you?

Most of the teachers I remember well were of the teacher-coach type, but I did once suffer through a class with an expert-bully. He was the last French teacher I ever had, in my second year of college. He had a formidable and brilliant mind, but held not much patience for students like me who weren't gifted with a perfect ability to mimic accents and learn the complexities of French grammar. I wasn't alone, though. He bullied even the best students, always finding some way to ridicule them. After that semester, I was pretty sure that I'd never enjoy studying French again.

# Influences

## *"Instant gratification takes too long." Carrie Fisher (Actor)*

Sometimes it feels like we've become a society of easy answers, pithy wisdom, and quotable bursts of insight.

I suppose it's just the inevitable change in information density that comes from advances in technology. The electric light bulb and the typewriter eventually led to the movie projector and the word processor. Readers begin to choose to watch 2-hour movies instead of spending days reading a novel and the next thing you know you're getting your news in 140-character bursts from journalists on Twitter. And who knows what will develop to replace Twitter. I surely don't.

When I was in college, there was a common slang term for the essential knowledge needed to pass a test or a course. That word was "nug," which itself was a shortened version of "nugget." If you asked, "What's the nug on Introduction to the History of Music?" you'd be told that the lectures were interesting but you'd have to commit "Wotan's Farewell" by Wagner nearly to memory to pass the final.

Now it seems that everywhere I turn, I see another "new" book by an aspiring teacher that claims to explain THE secret to success. And of course it's presented in five easy lessons, all reducible to a catchy acronym. I've got news for these writers. The "secret" to success is no secret. You develop outstanding skill in your field, work your tail off, and then if you catch a rare break of luck, you might succeed beyond your dreams.

Life isn't short and the wisdom you need to live well is not pithy or quaint. Beware the easy answer.

*"I would be most content if my children grew up to be the kind of people who think interior decorating consists mostly of building enough bookshelves."*
*Anna Quindlen (Writer)*

One Halloween I found myself interviewing for a high school teaching position that had opened up when a teacher had to retire for health reasons. Two days later I found myself teaching a class that had just begun to read *Jane Eyre*. I hadn't read *Jane Eyre* before then, unless you count the *Classics Illustrated* comic book version, which I'd read when I was sick one summer. I knew there was this girl, a handsome man, a madwoman in an attic, and a bad fire.

As you can imagine, I was poorly prepared to teach that class. For the first few days I could only do my best to stay a little bit ahead of the class. I survived, often by letting the stronger students drive the class discussions, but the students really didn't get their money's worth until after the following weekend when I read the entire book.

Being prepared in specific is important, of course, but I think it's also important to have a widely fed mind. One of my favorite English-Department colleagues from that same school was a man named Martin. He had not always taught English but had started his career teaching music. He conducted the student orchestra and directed the school's annual musical play. Always a wide reader, after a decade or so in the music department, Martin took some literature courses to supplement his college minor and got certified to teach English.

In that department we collaborated on tests and curriculum. One of the outcomes of this collaboration was a design for a final exam that I'm pretty sure came from Martin. This final exam was to be a series of four essay questions covering all the literature we'd read together during the semester. We designed the test to work like a Beethoven symphony.

The first question would be dramatic but somewhat straightforward. It would ask the students to comment on one theme from the semester. The next two questions would challenge the students to explain different themes from the literature, but in relationship to perhaps one other theme. In the fourth and final question, we made the students bring all the themes together in a synthesis of ideas.

This was a good strategy for assessment because it made the students grapple with the literature in new ways that they might not have considered, and at the same time would reveal how well they understood the books they'd read. They learned more even as they were completing the test.

I don't think we would have tried that strategy without the influence of Martin's knowledge of music. Living and reading widely will make us into better teachers.

*"Beware of the man who works hard to learn something, learns it, and finds himself no wiser than before." Kurt Vonnegut (Novelist)*

Ever run into someone who seems to have read every important book on a subject but can't deeply discuss any of them? I call these people résumé readers. They seem to be more interested in being able to say "I read Tolstoy," or "I read the original work on non-verbal communication by Birdwhistell" than they are in being able to apply that reading to their work. I used to make that claim about reading Birdwhistell, whose work was current when I was studying linguistics in graduate school. Here's the rest of the story.

How often have you read or heard the idea that 80% of all communication is non-verbal? It's practically a religious belief for some people. But it's also not true. For years I would argue with anyone who made that claim, usually by claiming the authority of having read the original work in non-verbal communication. Thing is, while it's true that Birdwhistell's original work does not support the 80% claim, that's not where the claim originated. So my claim of authority on the matter was false.

A couple of years ago a client insisted that my instructional design team include the 80%-of-communication claim in a training manual for line managers. I balked at including it, but I challenged myself to research the 80% claim in detail before challenging the client. In fact, what I found is that the claim seems to have started as a misinterpretation of some of the follow-up work on non-verbal communication.

That's how I learned that my usual rebuttal didn't hold water, even though I was right in principle. Now I can say that the claim is false and accurately say that I've read the research to back up my claim. I know that the original source was misquoted. I'm no longer that guy who trots out the name of a fancy scholarly work like it's part of his own résumé.

Besides, have you ever watched a foreign-language movie without subtitles? Did you really understand 80% of what was being said? I didn't think so.

*"A bookstore is one of the only pieces of evidence we have that people are still thinking." Jerry Seinfeld (Comedian)*

---

The bookstore is changing, or disappearing if you want to be more accurate. Borders bookstores are no more and I have some doubts about the future of Barnes and Noble as well. The days of there being a good independent bookstore in most towns of any size are long gone and it may not be long before we have a single national bookstore - amazon.com - that has no doors, coffee, or comfy chairs for reading. So, is this evidence that people no longer think? I certainly hope not. For sure, electronic books are the future but we'll probably have paper books for a few more decades.

Beyond the bookstore, we're losing the magazine and possibly even the daily newspaper. Or at least we may not have local dailies much longer and will read only the Wall Street Journal, the New York Times, and USA Today. Sad, indeed.

Are people not thinking any more, or do we simply have no common venues for the inspiration to think? It's the latter, of course, but more. I think that in the last couple of decades, at least in the United States, we've begun to separate into two peoples. One lives for intellectual challenges and growth and one mistrusts the intellectual life. This is what worries me, and I think it's what was bothering Jerry Seinfeld when he wrote (or probably spoke) about bookstores.

I think a society that mistrusts learning will create a dangerous world, one where the inability and unwillingness to do critical thinking will lead to decision making according to dogma. And that, as I recall, was a pretty good description for the Dark Ages.

We're teachers. Can't we do something about this? Isn't it our job to show that curiosity and learning are important parts of being human and good citizens? That's my take on it.

> *"It still holds true that man is most uniquely human when he turns obstacles into opportunities." Eric Hoffer (Philosopher)*

Hope for the future is why we learn and, I hope, why most of us teach. If we look around at our teaching colleagues, most are essentially optimistic people. As for the pessimists, I bet you don't admire them much as teachers, do you? The only truly pessimistic teacher I ever met was a man named Art. I ran into Art periodically when I was doing substitute teaching in the late '80s. Art was only a few years away from retiring and he kept a running tally of the number of days remaining to the day when he would turn in his grade book for the very last time. You could ask Art on any day how many days he had left and he could tell you precisely. He was a terrible teacher, too, as I recall.

I read somewhere that we become optimists or pessimists from the influence of our mothers. If that's true, then I'm truly a mixed bag. How about you? Was your mother an optimist or a pessimist?

My mother is an optimist at heart but she carries a hint of reflexive pessimism that may have come from growing up during the Great Depression. Shortly after I joined the Boy Scouts, I was chatting with my mother while ironing my uniform shirt. I told her that my goal was to become the youngest Eagle Scout in the history of my troop. Her reflexive response was to caution me against setting such a high goal because I might be badly disappointed if I didn't make it. She was being a mother, trying to protect me for sure, but I also picked up a note of pessimism as well.

On the other hand, my mother has always worked on her own personal growth. When I was in high school she took a night school class in decorative painting. That led to decades of enjoying the hobby of country painting, and eventually to her current role as a teacher of that art. I don't think that a true pessimist would have pushed herself to grow and learn as much as she has. For my part, I think that I may have converted that shred of pessimism into some lack of confidence. Fortunately, that's curable. My instinctual optimism, though, is terminal. And I'm glad about that.

*"Everyone has talent. What is rare is the courage to follow the talent to the dark place where it leads."*
*Erica Jong (Novelist)*

I learned about learning styles theory early in my teaching career. We were told that it was important to vary our instruction so that students with different styles could grasp our lessons in the way that suited them best. In recent years, I've also read that the existence of learning styles is, in the immortal words of Dr. Sheldon Cooper from the TV show *The Big Bang Theory*, "largely hokum."

There's a conundrum here - what to believe? I'm inclined to think that there are "horses for courses" in learning. When I took a break from teaching to make my millions as a stock broker (that's what I was "promised" anyway), I listened to many motivational and how-to instructional tapes as I drove to and from work. I'm not usually very good at remembering things that I only hear and I'm usually better at remembering written material.

Thirty years later I can recall many of the stories I learned from listening repeatedly to Zig Ziglar's tapes on salesmanship. Does this mean that I'm an auditory learner, after all? No. I think that I became an auditory learner in those drive-time lessons because I had to. With young children at home and a wife who taught full-time, I just didn't have any other time to learn from Zig except when I was in the car. Motivation and intention helped me switch to a different learning style.

Maybe this is a bit like linguistic code switching, where someone who can communicate in two different versions of a language moves between the two depending on their surroundings. Or maybe, we can all learn in any style if we choose to do so and have strong enough motivation behind our choice.

I never made those millions, as I'm sure you could guess. But I still remember something that Zig taught me through those old cassette tapes. "If you make lots of sales calls but you never ask for the order, you're just a professional visitor." Thank you, Zig.

# Writing

*"I have never thought of writing for reputation and honor. What I have in my heart must come out; that is the reason why I compose." Ludwig van Beethoven (Composer)*

Teaching has never been about the money, at least not if by "about the money" you mean that the amount of one's pay is one of the chief motivators for choosing that line of work. I think many of us got into teaching for noble reasons. We wanted to help. We wanted to make the world a better place. We wanted to spread our own joy of art or music or dance or business success. This is commonplace, almost cliché, isn't it?

Yet I think there's something quite powerful in going to work every day with the knowledge that your choice of work came from the heart. There's something quite intriguing about why someone would make this choice in an age of hedge fund managers making more than a billion dollars a year and maybe that makes us feel noble. Or maybe we don't feel so noble at all, and have left those dreams of doing noble work behind with our '70s sideburns and the big hair of the '80s.

Maybe our daily motives have shifted over time. Mine have. I remember that when I was teaching business writing in a community college, all I asked of the universe was to see just one cleanly written paragraph. Just one. That's not quite so noble, is it? Worthy, perhaps, but hardly world-changing noble.

It's been nearly forty years since I first stood in front of a classroom. Back then I really did want to make the world a better place - or at least give my students a chance to improve the world. Now, I worry more about inspiring growth and self-development. A friend likes to say that aspiring for change is pointless, because we don't ever improve ourselves from change. We improve ourselves through growth, and growth is where change can find its richest soil.

That's the kind of farmer I want to be. One who sows the seeds of growth. We're all farmer-teachers, in the end, aren't we?

*"Blessed is the man who, having nothing to say, abstains from giving wordy evidence of the fact." George Eliot (Novelist)*

This idea has also been well expressed by many people, including Abraham Lincoln. But I like this version by George Eliot. It speaks to the fire that must have driven Eliot to write, for as a woman (her real name was Mary Anne Evans) living in 19th century England she felt the only way to be taken seriously was to publish under a man's name. She indeed had something to say, said it well, and English literature is stronger for her books.

What you don't say can matter almost as much as what you do say. Comedian Jerry Seinfeld says that he will spend an hour to turn an eight word sentence into one that uses only five. At the same time, leaving out important details or important evidence to support your point will work against you every time.

For teachers, and maybe especially for speakers and trainers, there is a tendency to want to fill the vacuum of silence. We are talkative folks and often like to hear the musical majesty of our own voices (That's how I think of mine - how about you?). There's a funny thing about the human mind - it sometimes likes to spin new things around for a bit before deciding where to best store them. This is processing time, and it's best not to try to shove new information into the mind when it's busy processing something else.

Silence, perhaps offered up while moving about in front of the room for a moment, goes a long way toward giving all the minds in the room time to do their processing thing.

I'm reminded of a point made by a sales trainer who was leading a class in negotiating. he said that once an offer is on the table, the first person to speak loses. I suppose his point was valid, but it certainly was well motivated. Sales people - like teachers - are a talkative lot and sometimes you just have to shut up to let the prospect think.

When we lay down some vital new concept or a difficult idea for our students, we need to let them think it through. Let them come to the conclusion that they'll buy it on our terms and are then ready for more.

*"Drama is life with the dull bits cut out."* Alfred Hitchcock (Movie Director)

Nothing teaches more powerfully than a story. We devote hours to watching movies, reading fiction, and soaking up television dramas, and mostly it's all about the stories. Some stories terrify us and then end with relief. Others nudge us toward a better understanding of each other or how relationships work. And some are just all about making us laugh.

As teachers, we need to be sure that our stories accomplish our purposes. First, we should ask if the essential lesson in our story really is the same as the key point we're trying to teach. Second, we need to know if we're telling the story as economically and as concisely as possible. In other words, are there any detours in the text of my story that might take the listener away from my point? Are there any unnecessary words or phrases? And are there dumb redundancies like "Last summer, in July, my brother and I..."

Economy of telling is one of the chief arts of the storyteller. Listen closely to a good comedian tell a story and you won't hear a single extra word. Their time on stage is limited and they want to get as many laughs as possible in their limited time. They write with economy that we should all copy.

Hitchcock used to plan his movies so thoroughly that he rarely ever filmed alternative versions of scenes the way other directors often do. Other directors would wait until after filming to decide which version to use in the final edit of the film.

Hitchcock, instead, planned his films economically so every scene did exactly what it had to do to advance the plot, and nothing more. In our stories, every scene and every line of dialog should advance the plot or tell us something new and valuable about our characters.

In preparing stories for teaching, we should strive to achieve the economy of Seinfeld or Hitchcock. After all, what's more important - the sound of our own voice or the impact of our lesson?

> *"I write entirely to find out what I'm thinking, what I'm looking at, what I see and what it means. What I want and what I fear."* Joan Didion (Novelist)

There's something about the writing process that, once under way, frees up our brain to release its contents a bit more readily than usual. Sometimes when I get lost in writing for the pleasure of just putting words on a page (or a screen), the most remarkable ideas appear, ideas that I'm not sure I could have articulated so clearly otherwise.

This sometimes happens when I'm writing email messages. I write email replies fairly quickly when I'm working under time constraints and these quickly drafted messages sometimes contain the clearest expressions of what I have on my mind at the moment. Seems contradictory, yet it's true.

This is the best argument I know for writing out presentations in advance. I've often broken this rule and have given presentations from outlines. However, in practice, I've found that this approach really only works about half of the time. Sometimes what happens when I write out my presentations in full is that I'm reminded of good stories that I'd forgotten, yet they're just the right ones to support my points.

Another benefit has come from discovering that I really don't have fully clear ideas on a certain point, and then I have to wrestle with it for a while to get clarity. This is much better than making a fool of myself in front of an audience.

I know that teaching four different English classes every day or presenting for seven hours daily for a week means that you won't have time to write out your lessons to this level of detail. However, have you ever considered committing a few key arguments to writing - say the first day of the semester when you talk about why your students should give up food and sleep to learn what you're teaching? Might be worth a try.

> *"I love deadlines. I like the whooshing sound they make as they fly by." Douglas Adams (Novelist)*

It's tempting to teach before you're ready, to present a lesson before it's fully baked. How can you tell if an idea is fully baked? I think one of the easiest ways to do this is to present the idea to people who don't work in your specialty.

For this, you want people who are smart and articulate but not well versed in your field. If you can make your idea clear to them in just a few minutes (say 5 or fewer) then your idea is probably ready to come out of the oven and cool off for the frosting. If, instead, the questions they ask you after those five minutes are mostly about clarifying the substance of your idea, your idea might need more time in the oven.

This is one of the secret reasons for belonging to a Toastmasters club, by the way. Speeches given at Toastmasters club meetings are limited to a time frame, often only 5 to 7-minutes long, and every one receives a short spoken evaluation by another club member later in the meeting. If that club member didn't understand your new idea, you'll find out very quickly. It's an easy experiment to run, and you won't even have to make a disclaimer about harming no animals in the process.

You don't have to belong to a Toastmasters club to run this experiment. You could use your spouse as a sounding board, though after a few years of this he or she might be happy to see you join

Toastmasters instead. Not that I have any experience with this.

> *"You will never be alone with a poet in your pocket." John Adams (U.S. President)*

Have you ever marveled at how easily some people quote great writers? Or how easily some teachers seem able to paint exquisitely beautiful images with words? The first comes only from wide experience with reading deeply, and the second almost always comes from a life of reading as well. Somewhere in the depths of our brains, I'm pretty sure there's a system that's specialized for creating images and analogies to explain our ideas. And I'm quite sure that we build up this specialty system with wide reading of great writers.

Some of the teachers I most admire read great books regularly. One of these friends studies the great political speeches of the past like a scholar. Another is working on a rhetorical analysis of the writings of Abraham Lincoln. He recommends that teachers read James Joyce and Mark Twain to learn how to construct a strong story with compelling language. It's best to read the greats, you see, because they will always startle you, even after multiple readings.

Don't forget the poets, of course. Don't forget the poets. I recommend reading some poetry once in a while for everyone who teaches. Keep a copy of

Whitman's *Leaves of Grass* handy, or an anthology of poems. Then open it up once in a while for ten minutes to refresh your creative mind.

The great thing about reading poetry in small bursts is that you can almost always open a book to a random page and find startling new imagery or words used in surprising ways. Just as reading random wisdom quotes can trigger memories from your professional development, so too will reading poetry leave gems in your brain that will come back to you later.

So dine on Whitman or Keats or Shel Silverstein. And here's a bonus - you can consume all the poetry you want, for it's calorie-free.

# Your Turn

Now take a few minutes to let the following bits of random wisdom filter into your consciousness. What lessons rise back up to the surface? This is your random wisdom. Now put it to use.

*"Time is the best teacher, but unfortunately, it kills all of its students."* Robin Williams (Actor)

*"Only fools are positive."* Moe Howard (Actor)

*"I told my psychiatrist that everyone hates me. He said I was being ridiculous - everyone hasn't met me yet."* Rodney Dangerfield (Comedian)

*"I get a lot of cracks about my hair, mostly from men who don't have any."* Ann Richards (Former Governor of Texas)

*"It is better to confess ignorance than provide it."* Homer Hickam (NASA Scientist)

*"I loathe the expression 'What makes him tick.' It is the American mind, looking for simple and singular solutions, that uses the foolish expression. A person not only ticks, he also chimes and strikes the hour, falls and breaks and has to be put together again, and sometimes stops like an electric clock in a thunderstorm."* James Thurber (Author)

*"There is an evil tendency underlying all our technology - the tendency to do what is reasonable even when it isn't any good."* Robert Pirsig (Novelist)

*"To give anything less than your best is to sacrifice the gift."*
*Steve Prefontaine (Long-Distance Runner)*

*"You have to allow a certain amount of time in which you are doing nothing in order to have things occur to you, to let your mind think." Mortimer Adler (Philosophy Teacher)*

*"Winning is important to me, but what brings me real joy is the experience of being fully engaged in whatever I'm doing." Phil Jackson (Basketball Coach)*

*"I always wanted to be somebody. If I made it, it's half because I was game enough to take a lot of punishment along the way and half because there were a lot of people who cared enough to help me." Althea Gibson (Tennis Player)*

*"It is wonderful how quickly you get used to things, even the most astonishing." Edith Nesbitt (Poet)*

*"Everyone wants to be Cary Grant. Even I want to be Cary Grant." Cary Grant (Actor)*

*"Someone's boring me. I think it's me." Dylan Thomas (Poet)*

*"Without deviation from the norm, progress is not possible." Frank Zappa (Rock Musician)*

*"Health nuts are going to feel stupid someday, lying in hospitals dying of nothing." Redd Foxx (Comedian)*

*"Education is when you read the fine print. Experience is what you get if you don't."* Pete Seeger (Singer and Songwriter)

*"You have to know how to accept rejection and reject acceptance."* Ray Bradbury (Science Fiction Writer)

*"Music is the only language in which you cannot say a mean or sarcastic thing."* John Erskine (Novelist)

*"All great deeds and all great thoughts have a ridiculous beginning."* Albert Camus (Novelist)

*"Remember that as a teenager you are at the last stage of your life when you will be happy to hear that the phone is for you."* Fran Lebowitz (Journalist)

*"Mistakes are part of the dues one pays for a full life."* Sophia Loren (Actor)

*"My future starts when I wake up every morning... Every day I find something creative to do with my life."* Miles Davis (Musician)

*"Anyone can do any amount of work provided it isn't the work he is supposed to be doing at the moment."* Robert Benchley (Essayist)

# Index

Adams, Douglas ...................................35, 95

Adams, John............................................96

Allen, Woody .........................................59

Beethoven, Ludwig van...........................89

Benchley, Robert.....................................62

Carlin, George ....................................16, 34

Chanel, Coco...........................................15

Child, Julia .............................................13

Davis, Bette.............................................48

DeGeneres, Ellen ....................................23

Didion, Joan............................................93

Durocher, Leo .........................................25

Eliot, George ......................................45, 90

Fisher, Carrie...........................................77

Fox, Michael J. ........................................26

Fripp, Patricia..........................................32

Gladwell, Malcolm ..................................71

Hawn, Goldie..........................................19

Hitchcock, Alfred....................................92

Hoffer, Eric ........................................52, 83

Hope, Bob...............................................57

Jagger, Mick............................................49

Keillor, Garrison .....................................73

Klee, Paul................................................54

Kudrow, Lisa...........................................17

# Index

Marx, Groucho .............................................7

McCloskey, Robert...................................37

Navratilova, Martina ................................46

Obama, Barack ..........................................28

O'Connor, Flannery...................................68

O'Rourke, P. J............................................33

Quindlen, Anna .........................................78

Sagan, Carl................................................66

Seinfeld, Jerry...........................................82

Serling, Rod...............................................39

**Shelley,** Mary............................................7

Stowe, Harriet Beecher............................70

Swope, Herbert Bayard ...........................51

Tan, Amy....................................................40

Thompson, Hunter S.................................65

Thurber, James .........................................58

Vonnegut, Kurt .........................................80

Yeats, William Butler ................................31

# About the Author

John Labbe grew up in Augusta, Maine in a family that has produced several fine teachers across the generations. He earned his M.S. Ed. in 1974 and has been working as a teacher, trainer, and speaker ever since. A resident of Arlington Heights, IL, John provides speech and presentations coaching for entrepreneurs and business owners.

He is an active member of Toastmasters International. In the Toastmasters community, John has achieved the level of Distinguished Toastmaster and has served as a Division Governor in support of 30 local clubs. In addition, John has become a popular speaker, trainer, and leader. John is available to present on Random Wisdom Connections as a keynote speaker or workshop facilitator for private and corporate groups.

John and his wife Karen have three grown children: Jason, Emily and Matthew, who are busy building great lives. When he's not working, speaking, or reflecting on teaching, John likes to ride his bike, play golf, and putter in his woodworking shop. He proudly admits that he will never challenge for the Tour de France, is no threat whatsoever to Tiger Woods, and still has all ten fingers.

If you're interested in reading more about Random Wisdom Connections and more essays following this method, please visit the book's companion website **RandomWisdomConnections.com** and follow the Random Wisdom Connections blog.

www.ingramcontent.com/pod-product-compliance
Lightning Source LLC
Chambersburg PA
CBHW031325040426
42443CB00005B/215